I0504410

THE CUSTOMER-ORIENTED SUCCESS SECRETS FOR ENTREPRENEURS

CONVERTING LEADS FROM COLD TO GOLD

SExellency – Sales Excellency Series

GABRIEL HAYON

This book is dedicated to my wife Alicia, for her love and support.

www.wikisales.biz

TABLE OF CONTENTS

MY PASSION FOR METHODOLOGICAL BUSINESS SUCCESS

For more than three decades, I am escorting and running businesses. Some of them failed completely, others were in constant crisis, few – did well and the rest – had huge success.

In my research of those and other ventures, I wanted to find found interesting correlations, but, from the product and operational side, we did not find any affinity between the good and the lousy enterprises. Meaning that the product mix, manufacturing processes, inventory management and accounting systems cannot predict failure of success. I found great and lousy companies with similar products and processes.

The most influential factors in the Firm's destiny are:

- Sales, sales orientation and sales teams
- Clear Vision, Mission and Values
- Systems and Procedures
- Motivation, Ambition and Corporate Spirit

In the following chapters, I will reveal my roadmap, showing you the milestones.

My Sales Excellency Program will also show you all the pitfalls and how to avoid them.

WHY YOU SHOULD READ THIS BOOK

If you are managing your business or planning on opening one, Good Luck!

You will rely on luck. The odds are against you, as a huge portion of the new businesses is doomed to fail in the first year and much more may barely succeed.

If you wish to escape this dark statistic, you must do several activities in your business. This book, coupled with your hard work can place you on the roadmap to success.

CHAPTER 1: IDENTIFYING YOUR HONEY-POT

I am sure that, like me and most business owners, you struggled to find your Sweet-Spot – this elusive area that can skyrocket your Firm's results.

Let us start with an easy, but very important task. On the next page, please list your Assets and Passion

YOUR ASSETS

As part of your life experiences, you gained skills, certain things were learned, and you were exposed to knowledge. These are your Assets. Think of it as a combination of your toolbox and raw materials.

Identifying, understanding and listing your assets is the first step in this exercise. Please write your Assets below. For your convenience, I already placed several sample items.

Knowledge	Skills	Other
MA in Computer Science	Analytical	Driving License
MBA in Business Administration	BI Expert	Trilingual
Marine Technician	Extreme Sport	
Scouts Counselor	Sales Master	

YOUR PASSION

Unlike the previous section, here we are listing what we like and passionate about. Those are the things that are filling us with energy in the morning and that we are willing to spend time, money and effort to achieve or participate in.

Identifying, understanding and listing your passion is the second step in this exercise. Please write your passion below. For your convenience, I already placed several sample items.

Personal	Social	Other
Extreme Sport	Networking	Africa
Sales		
Robotics		

THE UNIVERSAL NEEDS

This third last list is more complex, as it can be as narrow as your town, segment or niche or cover the whole world.

The terms, Universe and Universal Rules, are borrowed from life coaching program and the Rules of the Universe. According to this philosophy, the Universe notices your efforts and interacts with you accordingly.

Identifying, understanding and listing what the Universe wants and needs are the third and last step in this exercise. Please describe those needs, pains, desires and thoughts below. For your convenience, I already placed several sample items.

Particular	Enterprise or Governmental	Global
Skills barriers	Competition	Hunger
Resources shortage	Lack of manpower	Corruption
Motivation	Poor training	Drought

THE APU MATRIX

Summarizing the three steps you did above into one Assets, Passion and Universe model, called APU Matrix is described below:

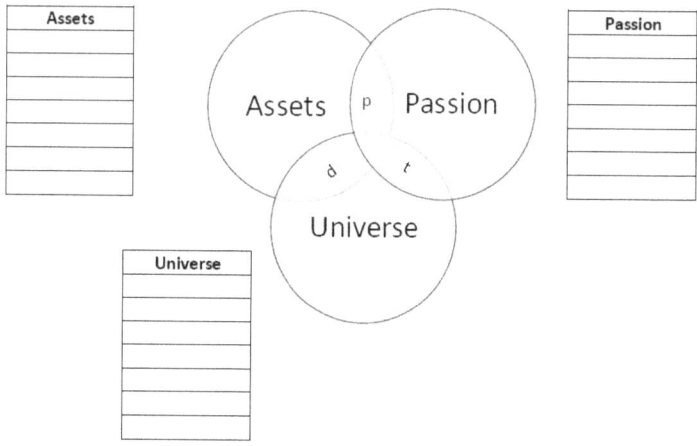

Take a free hour or two to meditate before continuing to the next step. This time of meditation will allow you to better digest and refine your results.

After filling the APU Matrix above, let's try to combine the results. Look at the overlapping sections in the diagram and notice the letters "p", "t" and "d".

"p" A niche composed from an Asset and Passion, but is not in demand of the Universe – will lead us a personal satisfaction, but also to...*poverty*. For example, your excellency and love of extreme sports is not a segment in high demand.

"t" When taking your Passion to an existing Universe demand, you will not have the skills and knowledge needed in order to succeed in this field. You may like African kids and have an urge for fixing cleft lip problems on those children. In order to gain good profit - you'll have to graduate as a physician and spend years in _training_ in maxillofacial surgery.

"d" The third overlapping section is a combination of your Assets and the Universe needs. For example, I am a certified aircraft technician and the demand for this profession is very high, but I hate the idea of spending my life surrounded by greasy spare parts. I may success in this field – but I'll be miserable. Reaching this section in the Chart will lead me to _depression_.

THE HONEYPOT

The area in the middle of the Chart, where all the three circles overlapping each other – is your sweet spot: it converges your best Assets, the topics you are Passionate about and that the Universe is demanding.

In my personal case: I identified my Honeypot in the combination of a set of skills in national competitiveness (Assets) + my love for Latin America (Passion) and the desire of the Continent to improve its international positioning in the World Economic Forum's statistics (Universe).

The term "Universe" does not apply only to the whole world. Your "Universe" can be extremely narrow. For example, one of my friends, connected his Assets (Languages, diplomatic experience, and organizational skills) with his Passion for alternative families and the GLTB communities urge to have kids. He is now running a successful surrogacy agency, assisting in the complex process.

YOUR OWN HONEYPOT

Now, with all the examples and tools described above, compare and match your own skills, desires, and needs of the market.

A good starting point can be with some needs of the market that you dominate that intuitively seems to align with your expertise. A good example is that of a friend who wanted to expand his local sesame seed paste – tahini factory. In the beginning, he thought to relocate closer to the sesame growing territories (hot countries in Asia and Africa), but after analyzing the market, he decided to move closer to the customers. He researched for the largest consumer group, with high Arab population density and determined that the best location will be New Jersey, USA.

So, while crossing your Assets with the Universal needs, eliminate immediately all the results that you are not happy with and keep only the ones you are really Passionate about.

Sample sets can be:

Assets	Passion	Universe based Honeypot
Portuguese + Engineering	Teaching	Rebuilding an engineering school in Luanda, Angola
Presentation skills	Kitchen	Video blog on cooking
Motion and Navigation systems	Kayaking	Training device for smart kayaks

List your own Honeypot here:

Assets	Passion	Universe based Honeypot

Observation

The term Honeypot is known as a synonym to Honey-Trap. This is not a coincidence.

Since we already established that your honeypot is related to your audience needs, consumers and prospects will feel much more comfortable working with you: as you dominate the segment and so passionate about it.

A good definition of your own Honeypot will attract customers' appreciation to your kindness, domination, great energy and empathy towards their pains.

Chapter 2: Your Unique Value Proposition

UVP, or Unique Value Proposition, also called USP in the Sales arena, is a set of ideas, vision, and values that will serve as your compass or GPS. A good definition of this set shall guide you correctly in your business, your personal journey and will force you to avoid unnecessary deviations from your target.

Vision

Based on the APU Matrix exercise and your personal beliefs, try to draft your Vision.

This is a complex task. It involves a projection into visualizing where your firm would be in, 3, 5, 10, 20 or 100 years time. I know about one family firm that has a vision for the next 10 generations!

Think about how would you like your business to be within one, three, five and ten years from today. If you are dealing with a trendy business, such as fashion or app development, make sure to include in your Vision also the development of future and alternative products that will never kick you out of the market. A vision for such company must include a statement about staying always proactive on the leading edge of the technology or contemporary design.

- **Oxfam**: A just world without poverty
- **Habitat for Humanity**: A world where everyone has a decent place to live.
- **San Diego Zoo**: To become a world leader in connecting people to wildlife and conservation.
- **Teach for America**: One day, all children in this nation will have the opportunity to attain an excellent education.

SAMPLES OF ENTERPRISE VISION STATEMENTS

- **Amazon:** To be earth's most customer-centric company; to build a place where people can come to find and discover anything they might want to buy online.
- **Nike**: To bring inspiration and innovation to every athlete* in the world. (* If you have a body, you are an athlete.)
- **Toys 'R' Us**: to put joy in kids' hearts and a smile on parents' faces.
- **Disney**: We create happiness by providing the finest in entertainment for people of all ages, everywhere.
- **Heinz:** The World's Premier Food Company, Offering Nutritious, Superior Tasting Foods to People Everywhere.
- **Ikea**: Affordable solutions for better living.
- **Starbucks**: To establish Starbucks as the most recognized and respected brand in the world.

TEMPLATES FOR YOUR VISION STATEMENTS

Personally, I like my declaration to be short, precise and focused, allowing growth in our volatile world.

Try to include a powerful and inspiring spirit into it as well.

Please dedicate some time in making your vision memorable.

DRAFT YOUR OWN VISION STATEMENT

To_____

_____

_____

_____!

VALUES

Values are a set of rules and boundaries you are enforcing on yourself and your firm, in order to be Cristal clear about your moral and ethics. It is knowing where and when to draw the lines.

It is obvious that all companies are expected to operate within the Law, but in this case, we are making our lives even harder. A commitment not to touch anything that is not moral, even if it is legal or a declaration to avoid doing business with certain people or organizations and even adopt certain best practices are part of such values.

In my firm, it is clear that I will not work with a firm that is involved in activities such as gambling, alcohol, tobacco or porn. I have rejected offerings from such firms, even knowing that they are operating within the Law. I will never link my reputation to an industry that is abusive (child labor, blood diamonds) or that discriminates (minorities, ethnic or gender).

Another example of drawing your lines is the following anecdote: While working for an industrial free zone, I recruited once a coffins factory. My boss rejected it, stating that it is a bad Karma.

It is essential that all your employees, customers, and prospects should be aware of your policy.

Placing you in a higher level than the competition is even good for the bottom-line, as it is eliminating the hassle with lousy businesses, that may manipulate you to gray areas.

Even more important and prestigious institutions are not likely to do business with firms that have sleazy brands in its client's list.

One of my partners in Chile negotiated a well-known multinational. During the negotiations, his firm agreed to desert a full product line just because its reputation was not good.

Another interesting example: while working for a software development company, I was in the final stage of assigning a promising distributor in Brazil for the retail market. In the evening, the CEO of the Brazilian firm took me back to the hotel. In his car, he had a nice selection of musical CD-ROMs. All the discs were pirated. At the same minute, I decided to terminate the negotiations with his company. If the CEO have no respect for intellectual property – his values cannot align with my firm.

List Your Own Values Here:

- _____
  _____
  _____
- _____
  _____
  _____
- _____
  _____
  _____
- _____
  _____
  _____

UNIQUE VALUE PROPOSITION

Your Vision and Values (V&V) have very little to do, if any, with your business lines. Those are like general terms, related to the philosophy of the owners and the corporate ethics. Those V&V shall survive even when your firm changes hands, product line, operational models, business models, markets or trends.

Once I founded a startup called Latin VoIP with a friend. In our Founders Agreement, we specifically wrote that our personal friendship shall be always above the business conflicts. This startup failed, but our alliance continued, such that even when things went sour with financial constraints and even when my partner changed his gender!

By the way, the V&V even neglects the shareholders and their pressure on the next quarter or value per share.

The UVP, on the other hand, is more vivid, very well connected to the product, market, trend, model, and financial targets. In most cases it is ONE (long and complex) sentence or paragraph, that dictates the targets in measurable terms.

MAKE *RUM* FOR SUCCESS

I like my UVP to be **Relevant, Unique** and **Measurable (RUM)**.

My favorite template is:

My Firm helps _____ that are struggling _____ in _____, to _____ in __%, by _____ within ___ months.

Enclosed two sample USP's written under this template:

XYZ is helping fleet managers to improve significantly safety, operational and fuel costs, by monitoring drivers' performance and vehicles' maintenance

WikiSales helps exporters that are struggling penetration to Latin America, to enter new territories and increase prospects in the pipeline in 30% by the deployment of local freelancers in the target territories within one to two-quarters.

In my case, I am even providing a guarantee of an additional month free, if we did not meet the targets within the agreed period.

Write your own UVP here:

_____

_____

_____

_____

CHAPTER 3: THINK STRATEGY

The term Strategy is derived from the Greek work *Strategia* – "the art of platoon leader". The meaning is achieving goals by deploying resources.

Strategy is, defining <u>objectives</u> and <u>goals</u>, dictating the needed <u>actions</u> to meet such goals, and <u>executing</u> the actions. A good Strategy is composed of strategic planning and strategic thinking.

In the last years, the term Strategy is overused for many non-strategic issues. Seldom, people confuses strategy with tactics, manipulations, and even operational staff.

The strategy of an organization should be the master-plan, linking the V&V and USP to the day-to-day operations. You can look at it as the large pillars holding the structure of the Firm or as the highway taking you toward the goals of the Company.

In this Chapter, you will be exposed to the powerful tool called TSAR Model. It is one of the methods to assist you in developing the strategic thinking.

WHAT IS "THINK STRATEGY"?

FLOODED BY THE CASH-FLOW

Most of us are living in our daily activities, from paycheck to another, and from petty deal to the next. This is what I am calling Flooded by the Cash-Flow: always doing the urgent tasks and ignoring the important projects. The same principle is applicable also to the way we take decisions. The time spent in a strategic deal is sometimes shorter than the time to decide on the next business trip approval.

This natural phenomenon limits our thoughts to the same level and we usually keep our performance in this small and limited frame.

The Think Strategy concept is to look at any issue in the wider and higher perspective:

- To ascertain the issue is important to handle right away
- To make sure it is aligned with the priorities and V&V
- To allocate the time and resources (not more or less)
- To see how the decision can affect the overall performance of the Organization

Think Strategy implementation serve all the elements of your business: any decision is measured in its impact on the V&V, UVP, and Branding.

Any deviation from the main strategy is considered as a non-supporting activity and must be judged in a critical form. My natural reaction is to reject detours like this.

HOW TO THINK STRATEGY?

So, if our Thought creates a Sentiment that generates an Action that produces a Result, we must **think on the highest and most sublime level possible**.

It is a known truth that "*if you think you'll make it or if you think you can't – you will be right in both cases*": if your thoughts are positive, it will grant you the energy, drive, and willpower to make it happen.

From the other hand, if you are thinking failure, obstacles, limitations – you will be right – and fail. Live according to the old but good phrase: *Aim for the moon. If you miss, you may hit a star.*

In order to obtain extraordinary Results, we have to start with extraordinary thoughts. In the following pages, you will see some guideline to set your own TSAR Model.

THOUGHTS

1. Think positively
2. Picture yourself in the position you desire to reach
3. Visualize in the most vivid way in this new status
4. Convince yourself that the position is yours

SENTIMENTS

5. Positive sentiments will start to overflow you
6. You will feel more energetic
7. Your self-confidence level will rise
8. Your body posture will change

ACTIONS

9. Plan on how to claim your ownership
10. Prepare your back-office: letters, messages, arguments
11. Link your pitch to the sublime vision of your audience
12. Present a strategic offer

RESULTS

13. Your ideas will be carefully listened
14. You will have the opportunity to open a dialog with the Top Management
15. You will be appreciated higher than your competition
16. You will take ownership of your position

From sales freelancer to C-Level Consultant

One of my mentees resigned from his job as a VP Sales in a software development firm. His goal was to position himself as a Sales Consultant and offer his skills as an outsourced vendor for other software houses.

- In our session, I showed him that a freelancer is like an employee, without the fringe benefits and that his hourly rate will even drop in comparison to his past position.
- The next stage was to elevate his energy level and change the direction of the business to be a Strategic Consultant in Sales for CEOs.
- We placed him higher and closer to the top management.
- He is now selling expertise and not executing sales tasks.
- As a Result, more C-Level professionals are retaining his services on a permanent basis.

From Mediator to Mediation Training Leader

Another mentee, an experienced lawyer and mediator, asked me to assist her in drafting a letter to the President of the Arbitration Center of her country. She wanted to be included in the Database of mediators on the Organization.

- After the TSAR Session, she offered her services to build and run for the Chamber's National Training and Certification Center for Mediators.
- The different mindset scaled her Thoughts, Sentiments, and Actions to a level that instead of being one more mediator in the Organization, she is building herself as an authority to other mediators, gaining much more knowledge, experience, power and money.

NEVER SACRIFICE YOUR STRATEGY FOR BUSINESS OPPORTUNITY

As said before, your strategy is your compass. Is shall always show you the correct way. You must keep in the same direction, whatever it takes and regardless of any obstacle.

While on this bumpy road, you will see some shining opportunities in the neighborhood: a tempting job opportunity, an attractive short-term deal or even a fresh business idea.

In some cases, such opportunities will arrive when you are desperate and willing to accept any income or grab any opportunity. This is the point where you have to show resiliency and hold firmly your steering wheel straight ahead.

Think carefully if this opportunity serves your strategy or not. Strategy Serving Opportunities are the ones that will shift you gently from the main heading but will improve your positioning, experience, knowledge, skill or exposure to the strategic goals.

For example

- If you are a marketing consultant and asked to join a social media marketing team – it will beef your skills and knowledge.
- If you are branding yourself as a local speaker and suddenly receiving an offer to lecture overseas – take it! Because it will help you to position yourself better and open you to more markets.

Now let's take the same two cases, with different offerings, that we should reject:

- The marketing consultant should not accept a full-time job because she will have to sacrifice her private practice and stop developing her own business.
- If the speaker wants to gain recognition in his region, he must reject an offer to be a ghost writer, because it does not service his strategy.

What Happened When I Sacrificed My Strategy for Business Opportunity?

Personally, my lectures to the general public are not highly paid. But it is a great marketing opportunity to my target audience.

By the end of any lecture, I am getting more business opportunities. Some of them are for in-company speaking, consulting, mentoring, and coaching, or to do business development.

All those opportunities are serving my strategy and all the products I mentioned are part of my portfolio.

On one occasion, an offer to do Biz-Dev turned to an Active VP Sales position and then to full VP responsibilities for two years. The payment was good, but it did not serve my strategy.

The time spent in this company took be back a couple of years in my positioning and strategic goals.

CHAPTER 4: FINDING YOUR BLUE OCEAN

Regardless of your business line, you must avoid competition almost at any cost.

W. Chan Kim and Renée Mauborgne, professors at INSEAD wrote the bestseller **Blue Ocean Strategy**, teaching how to create new market space where competition is irrelevant.

In the book, the authors are pointing that most of our markets are like red oceans: Full of competitors, fighting with similar offering to the same customers. This phenomenon causes them to reduce prices, improve offerings, giving more free services and features and invested a fortune in spying on the competition. This market cannibalization is leading everyone to bleed, painting the ocean in red.

For example, you as a customer cannot foresee the competitive advantage of the major laptop manufacturers such as Lenovo, HP and Dell.

One awkward way that competitors with similar offer are using to leverage, is by deception: in a negotiation with the three cellular providers for a corporate deal, I tried to compare the offerings, but the terms were not comparable, the calculation basis, penalties, data, voice, international minutes and roaming costs was so confusing that it was impossible to compare. The legal contracts in this case, are even vaguer and hard to make a calculated decision.

HOW COMPETITORS BECOME IRRELEVANT

The alternative to the Red Ocean is to identify smaller, less saturated niches. Those segments are usually too narrow and not attractive to the big players.

A wise analysis of this market will allow you to develop focalized solutions, catering to the exact needs of the Segment. Such a pinpointed offering is highly appreciated by the customers and they will be willing to pay a premium price for your solution.

In order to dominate the Segment, develop unique products, tailored to meet specific pain or need. Your clients will not be able (or willing) to benchmark you with the competition and price. This is how competitors become irrelevant.

FEW SIMPLE EXAMPLES:

ENGLISH FOR SPECIAL PURPOSES

The eLearning segment for the institutional market is very competitive. Cloud-based licenses are being sold for a few Dollars per student/year.

Due to the competition, developers must create more fresh content, add more features, update user interfaces, maintain high performance in the server-side and aggressive Service Level Agreements.

Prices are shrinking constantly and new competitors are raising all the time.

While managing sales to one of the leaders in the English learning market, we decided to develop smaller offerings to specific segments: *Medical English* – a short course for non-native English physicians, giving them the basic vocabulary and patient-doctor scenarios.

This course is priced 10 to 15 times higher than the General English Course. We used the same philosophy to develop Rural-Tourism course for small hotel owners, covering the interactions with reservations, guests, room services and concierge services.

An interesting story is that one of my distributors gained an English platform tender in the Ministry of Tourism because he was the only competitor that could offer a customized package for hotels.

PREDICTIVE AUTOMOTIVE DIAGNOSTICS

The Car tracking and theft prevention of vehicles is a very, very red ocean market. The sophisticated devices are being copied in East Asia, with minimal features, at very low cost. Cloud-based hosting and back-office apps are easier to get. So the entry ticket into this market is low, attracting more competitors.

The higher end providers invested a fortune in R&D to make more robust products and offering fleet management services to enterprises with large quantity of vehicles. Competition reached this segment as well, causing to shrink profit margins, before monetizing the investment in development. The ocean is very red. Many providers are giving away the hardware devices for free and basing the income model on the monthly service fee alone. This way they are increasing the financial exposure.

One of the companies in the segment, (that I was its VP), decided to take a completely different approach.

They hired a very good automotive diagnostics engineer and built a full array of mechanical alerts, keeping the fleet owner informed of any malfunction or even an evolving technical problem that is starting to develop in the vehicles. The Company provided the traditional tracking and fleet management capabilities as a "free" by-product of the System.

This way, the firm stopped struggling with low prices, fierce competitors, and shrinking profit margins.

The Service offered a rapid and clear Return On Investment (ROI) and we understood that the demand for the service is not price-oriented. As a matter of fact, we duplicated the monthly fees overnight and customers continued to enroll.

CHAPTER 5: BRANDING YOU

Regardless of what business line you are in, you must dominate your segment. In order to do so, you should start thinking about yourself as a Brand!

Change the perspective of your customers from being product-oriented to brand-oriented. In other words, your customer must stop looking at you as a product or service provider. You should be viewed as a *solution master* and you must brand yourself as one. This way, no customer will be able to compare to other service providers.

Generally speaking the term "Service Provider" is conceptualized as an external supplier of non-core help. Therefore, Service Provider is not strategic and can be easily replaced by another one. For example: replacing your food, transportation, travel agency, insurance broker or uniform supplier will not alter any of the Firm's results.

From the other hand, if you are well branded as a *Problem Solver* or *Solution Master*, the case is completely different. Most of us are not working with our hands, like mechanics, cooks or couriers. We are working with our brains. We are creating *Intellectual Property (IP)*.

Our customers are paying us to think for them, reach a conclusion, offer a solution or solve a problem, based on our knowledge, skills and past experience. But the most important ingredient is your *Critical Thinking*. This is your most valuable asset and your most expensive "product".

GABY – GURU > AUTHORITY > BRANDING > YIELD - PERSONAL SUCCESS PATH FOR IP CREATORS

Once we agreed that you are an Intellectual Property (IP) Generator, you have to justify your new position and support the brand called YOU. Don't be afraid to self-declare yourself as a Guru.

We live in a new world and we need no approval from anyone to proclaim our positioning. The author and guru – Seth Godin wrote in his book *"Permission Marketing"* that in the modern world you don't need any permission to publish. This book, for example, is a fruit of my mind. Unlike ten years ago, I didn't consult any industry leader or plead to any Lector of a publishing house to authorize the publication.

Like in other fields, in the Internet era, we are cutting the middlemen: the travel agent, insurance broker, retail stores, web-designers, bankers and the advertising agency. Today, social media allows us to reach virtually anyone, regardless of location, language, demographics or age. The only authorization we need is from the end user. So Permission Marketing is the fact that the target audience is interacting with me, reading my blog or opting-in to my mailing list.

It is your task to present yourself as a brand, but it is the Universe that should embrace you as one!

Therefore, your materials are paving the way to your recognition. The public cannot be fooled by phony or shallow reality-show stars. So be honest, sincere and generous with the content and materials that are describing you.

Talk about your personal life, failures, tell stories, share, interact, entertain and engage the audience.

Be personal, human, transmit honesty and avoid status symbols. By doing so, decide on the level of exposure you wish to give to your own family. Some are hiding and protecting the loved-ones completely, while others are sharing kids and pets' events. Personally, I am not hiding my family, nor placing them in the spotlights.

From the other hand, keep your online reputation clean. The best advice is to be in your Internet profiles in the way you would like to be seen in the real-life:

- Don't join groups that may embarrass you
- Don't approve anyone as a friend (feel free to use the unfriend option in Facebook)
- Don't like, share or comment, if it does not support your strategy and V&V
- Avoid presenting extreme opinions on politics, gender, sex, religion, race, etc.
- Keep a clean language

In the event that you have reputation issues from your past, there are several ways to clean it:

- Create a new profile and block all old ones
- Disengage from all your past activities and contacts.
- Ask Google to clean shaming mentions
- Use the service of an Online Reputation Agency

For your convenience, I created a short 4 step ladder to assist you to monetize your brand. It is arranged as my nickname – GABY:

The first step in your Branding Process is to convert you to a Guru – a well-known professional with a unique advantage in a certain field.

10K-HR - the 10,000-hour rule

Today, in our hectic and super-fast world, it takes some three years to reach proficiency and dominate your field. Three years of real work on a segment is equivalent to 10,000 hours.

Once you reach this period and really researched your segment – you gained the Guru status.

PyK - Packaging Your Knowledge,

Your experience, skills, and knowledge in its raw form – scattered all over your brain are not more than a bunch of gray cells.

Even if you try to keep track and document all your data in organized files – it is still not accessible to the public and to your clients.

In order to monetize on your knowledge, you must "package" it in an appealing format. Today, in the Internet era, you have plenty of ways to PyK:

- Book
- eBook
- Blog
- Vlog – Video Blog
- Website
- Articles sites
- Shared Dbases
- YouTube
- Paid/Free Content
- CD-ROM
- Subscriptions
- Newsletters
- Mail Shooting
- eLearning sites

Advanced tools like IFTTT ("If This Then That") or Microsoft Flow, allows you to replicate content from one platform to another. You can create receipts that will retransmit any YouTube movie to your Facebook, LinkedIn, Hangout, and Twitter, according to your pre-established recipes.

You can choose one, several or all the platforms. Most of them are free or low-cost subscription-based models.

Start with the free offers, see what works best for you and always, polish your content, approaches, and interaction with your audience.

From day-one, start building and beefing your mailing list. Due to anti-spam and junk mail regulations, be sure to obtain and record the opt-in permission. Most mailing platforms have this built-in option for asking and record keeping of permissions.

The mailing list will become one of your valuable assets. Keep it clean, organized and enriched with information about each prospect.

Never, but never, share your personal mailing list with others.

You can, however, as part of a joint venture or partnership, mail-shoot an offer of the third party to your audience, but do it wisely and not more than handful recommendations per year.

Create multiple mailing lists, segmenting it by professions, areas of interest, industries, and locations. I am keeping separate lists, even according to interaction level.

Products Portfolio

As any Knowledge Guru, you should have several products, at different shapes and price points.

The first important fact you must consider when pricing your IP – Intellectual Property is that the most expensive product in your portfolio is ... your time! Remember to think as a Guru and manage your time as your most precious asset.

General Public Offering

The second point is to rank your generic content and products to three levels:

Sales Funnel Stage		Price
Know – Teaser	Free report, Info, Open platforms	Free
Like – Entry Level	In-depth information, Generic knowledge	$3-100
Trust – Deep Interaction	Personalized Content, Unique Knowledge	$50 and up.

Please note that all those products are pre-packaged and consume little or no time from your side.

Personalized Products

As mentioned above, the next level of products is based on even deeper trust with your audience. And you can offer your most expensive deliverables to this selected group.

Those are your loyal groupies. They will follow you on all the social networks and will purchase virtually any new release. Such products can be:

- Group mentoring
- Personal coaching
- Mastermind groups

- Seminars
- Workshops
- Lectures

The prices of those product lines are subject to your understanding but should be expensive.

Some of my colleges have a "flexible" pricing model, so some customer will pay more for the same program.

Others charge more on days with high demand, and one of them charge more for shorter interventions. For example, if he quotes $2000 per 45 minutes lecture and then asked to do it in 20 minutes, he will request an extra because it is harder for him to do the "build-up" in so short time. Again, the main motive in this philosophy is that the customer is paying for value, not for time.

I am more open and my pricing is fixed for chunks of half-day. Meaning, if you are calling me for a lecture or a consulting out of the office, I am blocking the full morning or afternoon, even if the job actually took 30 minutes.

All prices are before transportation and accommodation. I prefer to arrive energetic and calm for the session so it is better to take a taxi (on the customer's expense) and not drive.

I am also doing small groups in my office, especially or Mastermind.

In those cases, sessions are "subsidized". It is effective for three reasons:

- Participants tend to consult privately on some issues, paying full price
- Participants are the best change agents and they will invite me to the firm or refer me to more customers
- As a captive audience, I am testing new methodologies and models on them, before the official launch

As a rule of thumb, always refresh, renew, alter and upgrade your top of the line products. This way the same group of followers will come again and again, feeling that they are getting more every time and not only repetition of the same content.

And, raise the price from time to time. I am giving my loyal customers to enjoy early-bird discounts, as a token of appreciation for their loyalty.

AUTHORITY

As a Guru, you have much more weight in your society and among your followers. Now, in addition to your knowledge, skills and experience, you are gaining more experience in handling your audience's needs and more power from the followers.

Your trainees, mentees, and followers will come to you with the most complex cases for your wise advice. They will also expose you to their customers and share with you the top decision makers. In some scenarios, you'll be called for emergency intervention, like crisis management or defusing a volatile situation.

You are now in the safe path to becoming an Industry Leader.

Be generous when sharing your knowledge. The more you share, more followers will fell that you have much more to give and the willingness to pay higher sums will raise. For example, when a client is asking for a quote, I will automatically give him a book or an eBook. This simple act of generosity opens the natural rejection and closing the gap between you and the buyer.

In some cases, I am doing a mini-session with the decision maker, touching some of his deepest pains gently.

Building a Sales Driven Machine

Sales1.0

In the ancient times, meaning, six years ago, we used to implement the old sales funnel going from mass prospecting and cold calls to qualified leads that after the demo will engage in a purchase.

During this period, advertising paid a major (and expensive) role.

Sales2.0

We have to understand that the old 3-feet rule (stating that you have to be within 3 feet from the decision makers) is not valid anymore.

The new rule speaks about 3 minutes – meaning that you should be available to your customers within 3 minutes, via phone, FaceTime, WhatsApp, Skype or WebEx.

In the new era, we changed the model. Basically, it is starting with social network prospecting, using technology, educating with quality content, while qualifying the leads, engaging and nailing the sale.

In order to effectively succeed in the Sales2.0, you must master the modern online tools. In this book, I will only expose you to the concepts and some of the tools.

Let me summarize some of the tools:

Free Social Media Platforms	LinkedIn Facebook Twitter Google+
Search and Social Media Paid Services	LinkedIn, Facebook Google
Leads Generation Automation	LeadSift IFTTT, ZAPIER
Leads Enrichment	Hoover's Datanyze LeadGenius Sales tools
CRM	SalesForce ZoHo HubSpot
Tracking	Signals YesWare Rapportive
eMeeting	WebEx GoToMeeting/Webinar Skype
Marketing	Eloqua HubSpot Marketo

Other tools to improve your remote business practice are document sharing platforms, eSignatures, presenting, mind-mapping and mobile interaction platforms.

Now, let's talk for a few minutes about online sales and sales prices:

I am dividing online sales into three large chunks:

- $0-99 small amount items, like eBooks and eBay/AliExpress merchandize. Buying habits are mostly emotional and not rational. This is why a $2.99 eBook sales much better than $9.99. Clients are impulsive and are not expecting to get premium service. It is an excellent idea to feature your open, upper side of the Sales Funnel with such products.

- $100-1000 premium goods. When spending such amounts, clients would like to take the products for a test-drive. Longer free demos are needed. But in most cases, a typical buyer will not surrender her or his credit card easily. They need something more. We can use all the tools in our arsenal; such as scarcity, limited time offer, testimonials, monkey business regarding pricing and even deep discounts – but in most cases it will not work. The best way is to use a "Success Officer". It is basically a phone call from a professional that can lead the customer through the process of playing, using the Products, but mostly is to give him the psychological support and confirmation that he is doing the right thing.

- $1000 & up   We can start filling the sales funnel of expensive goods and services, but we must escort the process, especially in the deeper, narrow side of the Funnel with personal intervention. Customers that are spending large amount have to feel good with the decision both emotionally and rationally. In our case, as IP creators, most customers will have to pass the full process: consume all the free stuff we have on the web, blogs, vlogs and articles, register for our paid webinars and seminars, buy our eBooks and books, CDs and DVDs. Only then she or he will be ready to do the big spend. Even in this stage, we must continue offering the money-back guarantee and no-questions-asked policies.

Customer Acquisition Strategy

In one of my early lectures to a group of startups in the initial phases, one of the participants lift his hand and challenged me, stating: "You are preaching for half an hour and yet didn't spoke about the Exit Strategy".

My response was: "Do you have Customer Acquisition Strategy?"

An Exit strategy is a term used in the phase that the founders are trying to sell the promising startup and cash-in. It is a pity that many founders are measuring success by the speed of exits, that is, selling the company and not in building a lasting enterprise.

Since we are in a business that we are planning on having for many years and leave it as a legacy for our next generation, we must think about how to get customers. Many of them, for longer periods and with multiple revenue streams.

If we wish to acquire customers for the long run, the first thing is to stop looking for the suckers with the deep pockets!

The second rule is to stop pushing toward the next sell and think about the long-term relations with your customers.

In one of my projects, I assisted one of the leading international shipping companies. The company suffered for years from the tough competition and shrinking margins due to a reduction of the international freight volume and the merging of some of the biggest brands. The Company was in a typical Red Ocean situation. The product was 100% commodity. All the companies offered the same price and duration to deliver a 20-foot container from Qingdao, China to Alexandria, China.

So we had to come with a differentiator. So we changed the typical slogan of "filling the nest ship" to Long Term Relations. This change is more than just semantics. It involved a deep cultural metamorphosis of the Company, from the Multinational HQ to the branches and divisions.

The customer Acquisition Strategy in this stage took all the client-base and started with a deep understanding of each customer, its needs; pains and gains, knowing the people, both in the inbound and the outbound sides, comprehend the business cycles, business areas, and routes.

By doing this we learned a lot about the sensibilities of clients. Just by asking the questions, some customers decided that since we care, they want to work with us exclusively. Other clients decided to give us an opportunity to participate in the bids. But the most relevant information was the knowledge about each enterprise.

Some are interested in more frequent routes to certain destinations, others told us about expansion programs that required a lot of freight jobs. We recruited clients that are very safety and security oriented, assuring them that we have the best practices and track record. Clients with an environmental agenda started to work with us as soon as they learned that we are doing the extra (500) miles to protect a whale herd and the usage of low-sulphur fuel.

In your SME business, a good starting point can start in the first exercise of the APU Matrix. In the Universe section, we defined our market. At this stage we can take the same analysis, and use the very same job done with the shipping company:

- **Due Diligence**: Gather information from the internet and other public-domain resources about the prospects, their business, locations, main goals, pains, gains and key executives.
- **Do "virtual interview"**: with your clients and prospects. "Ask" them why they chose you as a supplier.
- **Interests**: understand what the interests of your prospects and audience are. Some of this information can be gathered from an initial survey to be done with the customer.
- **Correlate**: if you know other prospects similar to an existing customer, you can extrapolate the data to this prospect.
- **Database**: take the information gathered, place it in your favorite CRM and arrange it as you understand.
- **Offering**: prepare an offering for your target audience. It must be aligned with your V&V and USP.
- **Reach-out**: go back to the Sales2.0 Section and select the methods that are suitable for you.
- **Traditional**: if you wish, you can deploy the offline and traditional marketing, such as free or paid lectures, seminars, phone calls, one on one interactions, go to networking events, spread the word at any forum, print-outs, business cards and brochures.

Hit the Basketball Court

I think that the best advice I received was from a former basketball coach that is now into business coaching. He told me that he can basket while sitting on the Bench. But it will not count. By the end of the session, he punched me in the chest stating: "Hit the Basketball Court". The message was short but crystal-clear: you cannot continue with theories and back-office. It is time to hit the court and play according to the rules.

Many of us are too timid in the go-to-market strategy and are not pushing enough to acquire customers. Your success depends on your willpower and willingness to roll your sleeves and sell, sell, sell!

ViViD Branding

Once you clearly defined the basic elements of your business, Vision, Values, and Differentiation, you can easily claim your market Domination and Positioning as a key player or opinion leader.

Now you are ready to package all the five elements of your Corporate Identity, also called Brand. Thinking about yourself as a Brand will change all your mindset.

I am not talking about inflated ego or phony cult of personality, but on a unique style. It must include a quite charisma, transmitting what you really believe in.

As a matter of fact, our domination and passion alone can pump you with enough energy to be very charismatic.

For a successful branding, it is recommended to build a Brand Identity. On the left, I placed my own logo, as a case study. I must admit that it took me less than an hour to design and execute.

Logo & Image
Your logo shall reflect who you are.

In my case it is me holding the Globe, transmitting international coverage and the fact that I am serving the Universe to my clients.

Color Scale
Red and black are strong colors, gold and black – for luxury goods and yellow/black are for industry and emergency.

The blue and light blue are meant for the air and ocean – the favorite colors of most airlines, transmitting internationality. The green is part of my commitment to the environment.

Motto

I recommend a shorter, easy to Memorize version of your USP.

It must be a phrase you can share and inspire your audience.

Fonts

Use an easy to read typography, don't go for childish, handwriting, too sophisticated or gothic fonts, unless it is part of your message.

Choose generic, commonly used letter set, because many exotic fonts will not look so great on all computers and mobile devices.

Other Visuals

If your business requires several icons or graphic elements, unify all of them under the same motive. For example, circles in red background and black image or drop-shape in light green.

Audio

Use an accent free, confident voice that represents you adequately. Either a female or male. The speed of narration must be the correct one for the audience. Faster for busy executives, slower for kids and elderly.

Personal

You can develop a unique dress-code. It should be clean, classy, aligned with your Industry and not flashy.

I strongly recommend avoiding banal or pathetic ornaments or gestures.

In most cases, a light makeup and business suit for her and a dark suit, well-groomed and a shaved look for him.

When you have doubts regarding the appropriate dress-code, the best advice is that "it is always better to be overdressed than under-dressed".

After having all the elements create your Brand-Book. This is a document that incorporates all the listed above and more, such as stationery, fonts sizes and letter templates.

Use the help of a graphic designer. Her or his experience will save you time and mistake. Since designers are using professional tools, such as Photoshop and Corel Draw, the job will look in better quality. You can shop online at sites like Freelancer or eLance. Fiverr is a great low-cost marketplace for designers.

Positioning

You cannot get positioning. You have to win it! Because Positioning is in the mind of your prospects and clients. Gaining Positioning is one step after you achieved Domination of your segment.

But, social media gives you the tools to obtain positioning: continue publishing in all the channels mentioned in the Sales2.0 section. The more you publish, the larger is your audience and the following crowd – the faster you'll position yourself as the Market Dominator.

Don't waste any opportunity to preach, speak, write, post or tweet on your subject. Get more and more people as multiplying agents to spread the word to a wider audience. If your segment is very small, you can invite them to a breakfast or social event.

Omni-Channel Leveraging

At this stage you should be very happy with your achievements: you have a growing audience, loyal customers, and followers, your entry and mid-level products are selling well and you are getting some high-level contracts from time to time.

You are well positioned and in full domination of your segment.

Now it is the time to leverage even more. Leveraging is a scaling-up game. You are going to use external forces to amplify your message and brand. Think of it as a ripple effect, of a stone falling into a pond. You are responsible for the closer waves and then your "levers" will do the rest.

Companies are doing it all the time. After domination of one segment, they are aiming toward another one. Hugo Boss dominates a share of the men's clothing. In its 2020 vision – they are targeting women's clothing, shoes and accessories.

- First Circle – Customers: The simplest way to leverage is to ask your existing customers to:
  - o Buy more
  - o To buy more frequently
  - o Up-Sale, Down-Sale, and Cross-Sale
  - o Refer you to other prospects.
- Second Circle – Look-alike: Then hit prospects that are similar to your customers
  - o Their suppliers
  - o Customers
  - o Competitors
- Third Circle – Affiliates and Partnerships
  - o Join Affiliation Programs as a Vendor. The affiliates will spread your message widely. The

affiliate has no commitment to a brand or a product and is interested only in the revenue share from your product. Smart affiliates are seeking high traffic segments, with costly products that can leave them nice income per sale.

o The major cost of the affiliate is in Google AdWords, AdSense, Re-Marketing and other paid advertising on the social networks. So in order to compensate for the investment on clicks without conversion – they must charge 30 to 60%.

o In some cases, the affiliates are scooping 100% of the first purchase.

o Look for business owners that are operating in a segment or geography closer to yours. They must have a product that is not competing with yours but complementing it.

o If you are a registered patent attorney, you can join forces with a Patent Writer or IP lawyer.

o I am an expert in International Sales, mainly in Latin America, so I partnered with marketing professionals, East-Asia specialists and organizational consultants. Each one brought her or his clients and mailed to their lists.

o In my role at the Chamber of Commerce, all our events are with partners on a territory or segment: The Export Institute, Manufacturers Association, major law and accounting firms.

- Fourth Circle – Go International:

o Identify players aboard that are operating in similar segments, again, avoid direct competition! Offer them to resell your program, under the same system you already developed.

o Part of the foreign partner job will be to localize the program and adapt it to his country's situation, legislation, taxation, etc. be sure not to surrender your IP.

  o In my case, I trained several partners in Latin America to deliver the Junior level seminars, leaving me the Senior level.

- Fifth Circle – Franchise
  o Once covered all those channels, you must have a very good working system, with all the controls and metrics defined. This is the time to write your operational manual. This guide shall serve as the bible of opening franchises all over the world.
  o Remember to check the franchising legal frame of each country you wish to operate, as it will have a direct effect on your income. You must lawyer-up properly for this stage.

Harvesting All Channels of your Knowledge (HACK)

If you reached so far, your journey is almost done. Congratulations!

Now you can place the business in auto-pilot. With all the systems in place, you should be able to make a lot of money without any intervention: The Internet sales from your sites, landing pages, affiliate programs, partners and other virtual knowledge products, will continue to feed your bank account. Maybe it is the time to spoil yourself and the family with a long vacation. Make a habit to review your sales every day to see that you are making more than the spending.

After the break – start to organize your wealth professionally.

On the business side – it is probable that some competitors will mimic your success and push offering into your segment. You may lose your domination if you'll not act proactively:

- Develop additional products
- Develop sequel products
- Make your program 100% eLearning
- Widen the market slice you already have by attacking other segments

As a full GABY Master, you must invest in yourself, your health, mental health and professional development.

Hire a great mentor to assist you with your multiple revenue streams and business decisions. Assign him also as a Growth Consultant for the next phases.

FINAL NOTE

If you are in your initial phases and don't feel that you have the "permission" to be called a Guru or that you did not reach yet your GABY Status, Then like many others:

———————————————————

Fake It until You make It

———————————————————

Chapter 6: 3D Success Model

My Personal Quest

For many years I delivered the Blueprint for International Sales. Results were not bad, but nothing extraordinary. I felt that "something" was missing in my training model, but I couldn't point it clearly.

When I turned 50, I took a series of coaching and programs and sensed the energy in the air. Then I realized what was missing in the Programs.

Most of them got very good product training before starting to sell but without one word about sales, handling objections or about the target market. So those fine people, some of them technician that got a promotion for sales, never attended one session on this art.

Most of my trainees in the International Sales Program were high-tech vendors. All of them, like myself, are computer geeks, from the faculties of engineering and exact sciences. They can relate perfectly with screens, keyboards, CPUs and servers, but not with people. Therefore, the communication method of choice was via email and chat. The most alarming fact was the poor motivation level of most salespersons.

At this point, I realized that I can fix it. By creating a program that will give a proper answer to all aspects of the sales cycle and beyond.

THE ROADMAP

The WikiSales International Sales Methodology is the core strategy in our Go 2 Market approach. It is composed of three dimensions:

Operational

The core of the System - the blueprint or flow chart of how to penetrate to foreign territories.

Energetic

Pumping and maintaining the motivation during long sales cycle deals and the passion for selling.

Mindset

Skill building geared toward moving the sales executive out of her or his comfort zone and the ability to adapt business models to a changing situation.

CHAPTER 7: THE OPERATIONAL DIMENSION – STEP-BY-STEP SYSTEM

OVERVIEW

Working with engineers, in any field, is a straightforward task. Don't waste any time with theories and overviews. Just give them the tools and let them interpret independently.

We love charts, graphs, statistics and flow-diagrams. It is so easy to understand, the sequence and the ramifications seem logical and friendly.

As an engineer, I am sure that you'll love and assimilate this Chapter. A focus on not neglecting the non-rational aspect – giving yourself a boost of motivation and inspiration at the Energetic Dimension and kicking yourself out of your Comfort Zone, is the Mindset of this section.

You will be amazed to see how much attraction you manage to get from your peers, colleagues, suppliers and clients. And, as a bonus – it will improve your family life.

BLUEPRINT

The Blueprint was the first methodology I developed, after systemizing my work as a salesman, manager and VP, managing and interviewing dozens of other sales executives and polishing it over and over again.

It is built for International Sales Executives. In the event that you are not a Global Vendor, adapt the model to your own reality.

- Developing winning messages templates and action-oriented mailing, as discussed above.:
  - Unique Selling Proposition,
  - Elevator Speech,
  - Packaging your firms' story
  - Prepare and test email templates for first, second and third interaction
- Due diligence properly before the meeting:
  - The firm
    - Check the stock status and trends
    - Get some financial data from open sources
    - Read the last year press review
    - Learn and memorize the V&V
  - The Industry
    - See how is the competition doing
    - Canvas the main competitors and positioning
    - Learn the Industry trends and major pains
  - The executives
    - Search LinkedIn and Facebook profiles
    - Find affinities with them
    - Look for political, religious, sport and business affiliations
  - Business lines and the share of each one

- Main pains and gains
  - Shrinking or slowing market
  - Macro and Micro Economic influence on results
- It is Showtime: engaging presentation: how to write effective presentations and how to deliver the message.
  - PowerPoint is (almost) dead! Most of us don't want to listen to long presentations, cut the volume. Think Twitter – 140 characters to deliver your message.
  - In most cases the 10, 20, 30 rule applies:
    - Ten Slides
    - Twenty Minutes
    - Font size 30 or more
  - Try to squeeze the full presentation to One-Pager!
  - Dress for SExellency: keep a clean look, use a dress code that is one level above the industry standard.
    - If everybody wears a long sleeved shirt and a tie – use jacket.
    - If a t-shirt and blue jeans – go for tailored pants and a polo shirt.
    - When on stage – Put on dark executive suite.
    - Light makeup and perfume. Shaved and groomed.
  - Present like a Pro:
    - Have your ideas clear, well-rehearsed pitch,
    - Message board with most scenarios,
    - Reply to typical objections
    - Master the audience with voice, tone, body gestures, pauses and eye contact
- Territories selections and research tools.
  - Map your territories.
  - Research all your territories by:
    - Macroeconomic Factors: Size, population, GDP Per Capita, technology / broadband / Internet / smartphone penetration
    - Distance from home

- Micro-Economic Factors: relevant to your industry: child mortality rate, hospital beds, literacy rate, Android Vs. iOS, paved roads, skin cancer vulnerability
  - Rank the selected Territories by Likelihood to Purchase. You may need to factor each criterion.
  - Eliminate the last ones
  - Focus on the highest five territories
- The art of segmentation: Maximize your sales in each territory
  - Slice the target territory. Basic segments are:
    - B2G - Institutional, including Government, federal, state, municipal, provincial, regional, academies, churches. In some cases – NGOs
    - B2B – Enterprise, Corporate, SME, private sector, for-profit institutions, distributors, agents and sales channels
    - B2C – retail, consumers, end-users, channel marketing to mass market, individuals, mom & pop shops, affiliate marketers, SOHO
  - Pinpointed market research tools, as described in the Sales2.0 Section.
- Drill-down in the selected segment. This is your way to dominating also the customer's arena and territory. It will give you huge leverage over your competitors and improve your positioning in the eyes of the clients as a real professional.
  - Main players,
  - Competitors
  - Prospects landscape
  - Barriers
  - Regulatory issues

- By doing so you will be able to convert your customer's environment to your own playground. And converting his competitors to your prospects.
- Virtual Ping-Pong: negotiation with prospects.
  - Use the knowledge you gathered wisely
  - Deploy your own negotiations strategy and tactics. Sequel to this book, I will include a Chapter on Power Negotiation.
  - Aim toward the highest common denominator: the decision maker and her or his influencers
  - Checklist for closing-readiness and willingness.
- Draft the agreement
  - Make sure to close all issues verbally, even before you travel to meet the prospect, and that all his questions and issues have been solved.
  - Send him a Business Terms Sheet. This is a one-pager document, summarizing all the commercial terms (products, rights, services, prices, quantities, etc.), without the intimidating legal part.
  - Once both parties agree to the Terms, you should ask for an LOI – a Letter of Intent, confirming his approval of the Terms.
  - Now you are ready to travel.
- Defusing conflicts with your partner
  - Conflicts and disputes are very common in commercial relations between the partners. Make sure to keep the disagreement contained.
  - Stay focused on the problematic issues only
  - Never, and never, move the conflict to personal track. It is a business and should be kept as thus.
  - Keep your friendship with the person on the other side, especially if you have to be the "bad cop".

- o Record all verbal understandings in your own words and obtain the approval of the partner.
- Instant Sales: how to close the sale on the first meeting?
  - o The typical B2B model of long sales-cycle deals is long and involved several trips overseas of several team members.
  - o Several years ago I streamlined the Process to six interactions and three meetings, over several months.
  - o Since it is still too long, I started to use advanced Internet tools to communicate, interact, educate, collaborate and engage remotely.
  - o As a matter of fact, a large part of the process can be done by a junior sales executive or marketing coordinator.
  - o Now I am preparing everything, including the legal paperwork in advanced, and the face to face meeting is to nail the deal, shake hands and use the momentum and enthusiasm of the newly assigned partner to start a training and visit end prospects.
  - o This is a very powerful confidence-building instrument, as the partner sees you as his ally in getting more deals and monetizing on his investment.
- Events, fairs, and conventions: lead and let Marketing sweat!
  - o Tradeshows and other industry events have the wrong perception for most entrepreneurs. Many see it as an opportunity to launch new products, to see what new and generate some leads, while drinking cocktails.
  - o My understanding that those events are the most important days in the lifecycle of the firm: in three days of a fair you can meet more prospects than a full year!
  - o Therefore, a trip must be planned many months ahead.

- o You have to leverage on all the events, advertising, speaking and award opportunities.
- o Use the exhibition days to meet as many prospects as you can. Rank them and follow up as soon as you can.
- o Keep track of your prospects and keep them informed of your news.
- o Take the time to gather competitive intelligence on your rivals
- o The full manual will be launched later this year in the sequel of the SExellency series.
- Inter-culturalism: develop an ethical and politically correct conduct with foreign cultures.
  - o As most of your interactions are international, you will face different cultures. Some of the habits are related to the habits of the locals. For example, in many societies, such as the Latin and the Chinese, it is rude to have confrontation and give negative, so those people will avoid it at all cost.
  - o Recently, the Harvard Business Review published a business model called Getting to Si, Ja, Oui, Hai, and Da, that is mapping nations in two axes: the emotional Expressiveness and the Confrontation Style. Understanding each nation's negotiation style can help you to cut the persuasion time and adapt it to the audience's habits.

Emotionally Epressive

Israel
Russia   Italy   India   Saudi Arabia
France   Spain   Brazil   Mexico
                                          Philippines

                      USA

Confrontational ————————————————————————— Avoid
                                                      Confrontation

         Holland   UK
            Denmark
Germany   Sweden
                                 Korea
                                      Japan

Emotionally Unepressive

CHAPTER 8: THE ENERGETIC DIMENSION – A FULL TANK OF MOTIVATION

In the beginning of Chapter 6, I mentioned the motivation issue among sales executives briefly. The truth is that it is a major problem.

Many salespersons were so frustrated from constant rejections that they stopped approaching new customers and focused only on the existing ones.

In some cases, I requested to see call logs and found out that a large share of them didn't make one outbound call for days.

Without a clinical background in psychology, I could evidence levels of depression among them. Later on, I even used the cold-calls as an index to the resiliency and temper of salespeople.

A good outbound sales agent, that have to do 50 to 60 calls per day, and reach around half of it, must know that only 10% can be converted to buyers – less than three per day. Therefore, they must accept negative answers as part of the day.

I teach them to embrace the rejections and objections: a prospect that declines my offer – he is actually saving me precious time, that can be dedicated to the next call. All my mentees are thanking those prospects.

Regarding objections – most of them are not even objections but signs showing that the prospect is trying to make a statement, others need more assurances that they are about to take the right decision, some are presenting fear of a change, extra work or to be under control of the new system.

Price objections are looked today as a readiness signal. If a customer claims that the product is too expensive – his inner voice is saying that he'll buy if the price is correct.

This is the opportunity to ask if this is the only issue, and if fixed – he will purchase.

By the end of this training, the coordinators and telemarketers understand better the buyer side of the equation. They are learning how to improve closing, reduce time with unqualified prospects and accept that rejections are fine.

Another motivation booster is to celebrate each closed deal, the sales agent of the day, best performer, highest volume and the outstanding team.

In long sales cycles deals, we can celebrate "Little-Wins" with each step deeper in the sales funnel: approval of pre-sale session, coordination of a demo, execution of a pilot, successful PoC (Proof of Concept) and setting a meeting with the decision maker.

Polishing constantly, Kaizen-like, of your call scenarios are helping agents to focus on the target, cut the qualification and closure time, lead prospects to more up sales, down sales and cross sales.

All those tasks are pumping and maintaining the motivation during the sales cycle and boosting the passion for selling.

THE TSAR – THOUGHTS ACTUALLY CREATE REALITY

One of the Rules of the Universe is talking about the Magic Circle. Our Thoughts (high or low, powerful or lame) are generating corresponding Sentiments (positive or negative, elevating or depressing). The Sentiments are inspiring us to take Actions (Good or bad, big or small). The Actions are creating Results.

The quality and the magnitude of our Results are, therefore, directly linked to our Thoughts. These Results are feeding our Thoughts and so on.

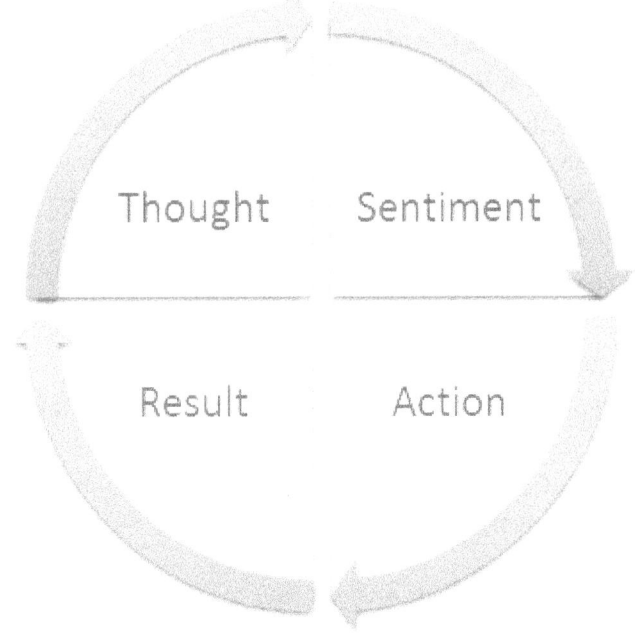

Thought   Sentiment

Result   Action

THE LAWS OF THE UNIVERSE

If the TSAR is the trigger of the human operating system, the Laws of the Universe are more global and less obvious. You are not expected to believe or obey the Rules. Even the number of rules are not clear. In the next lines I am simply listing the seven most basic ones, just for general knowledge:

- **The Law of Resonance** helps you to think and meditate of the correct "Vibe" of what we want to achieve and therefore – attract it. The Law of Attraction, from the bestseller "the Secret" is part of the Resonance Law.
- **The Law of Relativity** is applicable for cases that we have to relate to things in order to maximize them. Combining random facts to a full picture.
- **The Law of Cause and Effect** states that for every action, there is an equal and opposite reaction.
- **The Law of Polarity** states that everything has an opposite. Hot-Cold, Light-Dark, Up-Down, Good-Bad. Our goal is to find the balance between the opposites.
- **The Law of Rhythm** states that everything has a natural cycle, beyond our influence.
- **The Law of Gestation** states that everything takes time to mature.
- **The Law of Transmutation** states that energy moves in and out of physical form.

My basic knowledge of the Rules is that part of my mission is to give. Giveaway, my knowledge, methodologies, share information, assist in networking, guide, coach and mentor. My belief is that by giving, the Universe will reciprocate and compensate me in one way or another.

Luck = Opportunity X Readiness: How to Harness the Laws to Your Success

When looking as a successful person, the first intuitive thought is that she or he is so lucky.

The truth is that most luck is seasoned with a lot of sweat.

Being successful is not grabbing opportunities because all of us will encounter many business opportunities.

So, why is it that the "successful one" are always managing to take advantage of such opportunities?

The simple answer is that they **prepared** all their lives for such opportunity!

The definition of the so-called Luck is ***"Opportunity that Meets Readiness"***.

I will phrase it mathematically:

Luck = Opportunity X Readiness

The meaning is that zero readiness will automatically lead to zero success!

Our readiness is the sum of all our Assets: experience, knowledge, and skills, together with the right Mindset, (see next Chapter) and the right Energetic level.

The Rules of the Universe are speaking about wealth and abundance that are flowing toward us all the time. In our day-to-day language – those are the business opportunities that are appearing from time to time.

Traditionally, we are ignoring some of those opportunities and we fail to see others.

Part of this negligence is fine. Especially if the Biz Op is out of our core competence or not aligned with our V&V.

Only when we are truly ready physically, mentally and equipped with the right set of skill, experience and knowledge – we will be able to harvest the opportunity effectively.

FULL TANK OF ENTHUSIASM, PLEASE: HOW TO KEEP THE MOTIVATION FLAME

The life of any entrepreneur is not easy. Working from SOHO – Small Office / Home Office without any friends, peers or colleagues, you'll find yourself very lonely. You will need someone to consult with. Personally, anytime I faced a challenge, I went to consult with the… refrigerator.

You will also need a support system to assist you in tasks you are not trained or not good at, such as accounting, graphic design, translation or Marcom. We must be multitasking and expenditures experts.

Furthermore, you shall have someone set your goals, objectives, and due dates, just like your old grumpy boss.

Long working hours and too far light in the end of the tunnel are the last piece of the Solopreneur.

Therefore, it is essential to control your energy levels. When asked if I can give one advice to a SOHO owner it will be:

Keep your Burn Rate Low and Your Spirit High!

It is so important to balance and master both aspects – the money spending and the motivation, that I developed a full program once just for this purpose.

The financial issue can be tackled by using Lean Startup methods. Today, the entry cost to the SOHO business is relatively low: you can lease and not buy expensive computers, printers, and servers. Use cloud services and expand to the maximum the free or entry level offering of the service providers such as accounting, mailing, CRM, ERP and website.

Use minimal payments, delay payments to providers to the bearable level and be more aggressive with your collections.

Try to refinance, take a second mortgage and minimize on your car expenses.

The motivational issue is a bit more complicated. From my period in the high-tech, I learned that it takes on an average 3 months to convert a cold lead to a distributor, 2 more months in training, 3 more in his prospecting and 3 to close the first deal. Give him 2 more months for implementation and 2 last months to pay. A Total of 15 months, meaning that I will see the commissions in my paycheck only 16 months after starting the process.

With such a long period, our energy levels are draining constantly. In order to assure that it will not happen to you, first, understand the process and be even more conservative in your projections.

Divide the long process to small chunks. Set due date for each step and celebrate each achievement.

Another wise advice is to start interactions with "Low Hanging Fruits"- customers that are easier to close. This will do good to your back account and your spirit.

Build a pipeline with several different products for a variety of clients, so you will not depend on one product, customer or timeline.

Light sport is also a great motivator. Make yourself a habit to add some physical activity to your agenda. My favorite is walking in a rural area early morning. It pumps my adrenaline level for the first hours of the day.

Some people love to do yoga or other spiritual activity, like praying. If it helps you – great.

Don't let your family or business partners, suppliers and customers feel that you are not motivated.

Find a good friend, or if needed a therapist to share your thoughts and sentiments.

A Mastermind group can be a good motivator, as most of the participants also passed lower levels of energy and they will assist you in "cooping" it.

While commuting – make a habit of listening to motivational speakers and cheerful music or even a comedy. Avoid the news or any negative vibe source.

Stop meeting your depressing friends and family. If they are not contributing to you – avoid them!

ADAPTATION FOR BELIEVERS - THE SPIRITUAL DIMENSION

In my experience with religious communities, mainly evangelists, we linked the Energy and Divine Spirit together, as the Spiritual Dimension.

If it works for you – consider connecting your beliefs and entrepreneur motivation. It will definitely guide your positive motivation flow.

HANDS-ON: PERSONAL GOALS SETTING SESSION

As mentioned earlier in this chapter, a wise idea is to split your main goals into smaller mini goals attaches to the "little wins" in the process.

As an engineer – I recommend treating the Goals as Projects with defined deadlines. You can use a project management software or a Gantt to record your goals.

Start with the big picture – your strategy.

Cut it to main objectives: the pillars of your strategy, such as: build the website, launch a product, send the first newsletter, compile mailing list, publish an eBook and so on.

Now cut each Goal into tasks. The eBook project, for example, can be divided into topic research, keyword research, niche identification, topics drafting, writing the content, editing, designing the cover, compiling, publishing and marketing.

Set start and end dates for each task. Celebrate each step and rush yourself with the delays.

Goal	Task	Start	End	Timeline							
				W1	W2	W3	W4	W5	W6	W7	W8
eBook	Research	Jan 1	Jan 7	�							
	Keyword	Jan 1	Jan 7	▪							
	Niche	Jan 1	Jan 7	▪							
	Draft	Jan 7	Jan 14		▪						
	Write	Jan 7	Jan 28		▪	▪	▪				
	Edit	Jan 21	Feb 5			▪	▪	▪			

CHAPTER 9: THE MINDSET DIMENSION

The third dimension is my own secret ingredient. In my years in all positions on the executive ladder, I learned that people are avoiding changed whenever they can.

In this Chapter, we will discuss the skill building geared toward moving the entrepreneur and sales executive out of her or his comfort zone and to gain the ability to adapt business models to a changing situation.

WAKE-UP CALL TO YOUR AWARENESS

Listening to peoples' excuses for not doing something is a frustrating and annoying task.

It is always about the "situation", the economy is too slow, the stock exchange is too high, I am too old for this, I am too young for this, I don't have the knowledge, I am overqualified for this, I am not from the right family, gender, color, race religion, etc.

Those are excuses that we are telling to yourself. Recently, I offered an old friend to represent an educational technology firm in his Central American country. Before he opened his mouth, just from his body language and facial expression, I understood that he is going to lecture me that it will not work. Half an hour later and one block away, I closed the deal with a better entry point to a younger firm.

Breaking your own boundaries must be a priority in our training. Developing a mindset stating "I can do it", is a winning virtue. Today, in the startup arena, most investors are not looking for the successful ones, but asking the entrepreneurs about their failures. Understanding that even if the venture failed – the knowledge is conserved and the next time it will be better. In the last year a new convention has been launched – FailCon. This is a gathering of startup founders that are openly speaking about the failures they had and how it prepared them to be better entrepreneurs in the next venture.

KICKING YOURSELF OFF YOUR COMFORT ZONE

It is a natural habit to stay closer to sets of safety boundaries.

For example, most export-oriented companies are aiming toward the US market. When asked, they'll tell us that is thanks to the huge size of the consumer market. But the truth is that they feel more comfortable to work in a known language.

When diversifying beyond the English-speaking countries, USA, UK, Canada and Australia, they'll go to the Western Europe, because of the solid legal frame.

The real reason behind the decision to stick to those territories in the two examples is our natural desire to stay within our Comfort Zone.

But due to the same fact, those segments are very saturated with competitors. So the customers are pickier and more price conscience. Since we are talking about sophisticated market – the "First World", the quality standards are also very high and the entry barrier is extremely challenging.

The real opportunities are in the developing and emerging markets: South East Asia, Africa, Latin America and Eastern Europe.

Seth Godin took the Comfort Zone to a more embarrassing level: he is saying that in tough situations, our Lizard Brain kicks in and controlling our activities and decisions. This is the most primitive part of the brain, responsible for our survival. The good news is that we can train our modern brain to overcome the amygdala, just like firefighters are running toward the fire, while everyone in escaping out.

Once you'll learn to work in the less organized and civilized part of the world, you'll start enjoying it. Profit margins are better, customers are less demanding and you'll feel in an adventure.

IDENTIFYING NARROW, YET PROFITABLE NICHES & OUT-OF-THE-BOX OPPORTUNITIES

We spoke about this point briefly earlier. Part of the success is the ability to dominate the market. Yes, I am aware that for a small entrepreneur from a little town, it is very hard to achieve superiority in any segment.

But, if you'll identify a small, neglected niche that other providers are not interested in – own it! You can research it, explore it, learn how are the major players, barriers, competitors and regulation and within a short period of time – obtain a full domain of this segment.

The field of vocational training is dominated by a handful of strong factories that are manufacturing all the simulators. The devices are big, robust and extremely expensive. One of my customers developed similar training boards. His systems are not as fancy as the traditional ones but have two main advantages: using industrial grade components that the school can purchase at any local hardware store and a very competitive pricing.

Since the larger suppliers neglected the poor vocational schools, including the government-owned academies, we managed to penetrate into this niche. We learned the competitors, pricing, gave free training sessions to the teachers and within one year – we concurred the low-cost segment.

FLEXIBLE BUSINESS APPROACH

When approaching your clients, either face to face or remotely, it is important to come open-minded. This is another facet of your mindset.

In many cases when proposing to customers, they will try to change the scenario. The reasons can vary, which may be the desire to lower the price or improve conditions, corporate restrictions that limit them from accepting the offer and a rejection of the proposal.

In all those cases, you can modify your offering in order to adapt it to the buyer's needs:

Objection	YOUR RESPONSE
Desire to lower the price or improve conditions	Tradeoff: "if I'll get you the Discount / Conditions – will you sign the PO today?"
Corporate restrictions that limit them from accepting the offer	Come to the negotiation table with several business models. "If you can't purchase, can you agree with our recurrent monthly payments?" "I understand that you run out of budget for this year. If I supply the Product/Service now, will you place the PO with payment commitment for January 1st?
Rejection of the proposal	"You told me you liked the Product. What can I do for you to have the product today?

ADD YOUR OWN INGREDIENTS

- _____
  _____
  _____

- _____
  _____
  _____

- _____
  _____
  _____

- _____
  _____
  _____

ABOUT THE AUTHOR

Gabriel Hayon is an International Sales Guru, National Competitiveness Expert, Business Facilitator, International Speaker, Mentor & Coach. Gabriel Speaks Spanish, English, Hebrew and Portuguese.

- Review Gabriel's LinkedIn Profile
- Gabriel's Facebook
- Training & Consulting http://www.wikisales.biz/
- Other Publications by Gabriel Hayon
- Contact Gabriel gabriel@wikisales.biz
- Order additional materials, lectures and seminars